Let's Play Tag!

 Read the Page

 Read the Story

 Repeat

 Stop

 Game

Level 1   Level 2   Level 3

I SPY ™
IMAGINE THAT!

Illustrations by Walter Wick
Based on riddles by Jean Marzollo

SCHOLASTIC INC.

I spy a spoon, a chair, a clock,

A fork, a mouse, and a fish on a block.

 I spy a magnet, a plane to fly,

A one, a cat, and the sun in the sky.

I spy a hat, a kite, a moon,

A ladder, a ship, and a small balloon.

 I spy a crown, a snake, a B,

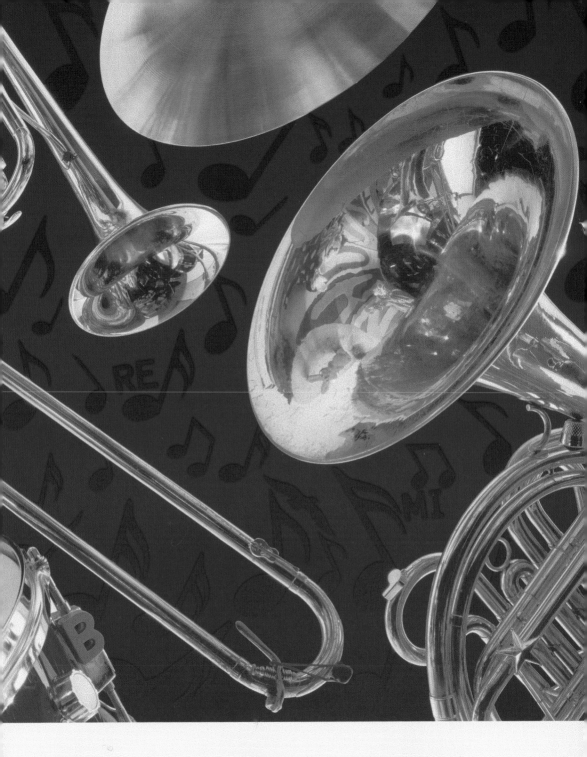

A whistle, a star, and DO RE MI.

I spy a cake, a teapot, a chair,

A tiger, three cars, and a panda bear.

I spy a ladybug, a feather that's blue,

An acorn, a seashell, and the number two.

I spy a door, a penny for a wish,

A turtle, a book, and three starfish.

I spy a caboose, a lock, a key,

A horse for chess, and a horse from the sea.

purple

yellow

red

green

orange

blue

helicopter

car

truck

train

On The Move

plane

bus

boat

motorcycle

21

acorn

moss

seedpod

clover

pinecone

honeycomb

Nature Walk

petal
gourd
turquoise
mushroom
dragonfly
bark
binoculars

r i n g

bee

d o g

bat

c a t

K

k i n g

tree

star

frog

bell

moon

shell

spoon

car

25